ORIGAMI

ARCTURUS

ARCTURUS

This edition published in 2019 by Arcturus Publishing Limited
26/27 Bickels Yard, 151–153 Bermondsey Street,
London SE1 3HA

ISBN: 978-1-78428-231-8
CH004287NT
Supplier 13, Date 0619, Print Run 8785

Models and photography: Belinda Webster, Michael Wiles & Jessica Moon
Text: Lisa Miles & Jennifer Sanderson
Design: Jeni Child
Editors: Becca Clunes, Kate Overy & Joe Fullman

Printed in China

Contents

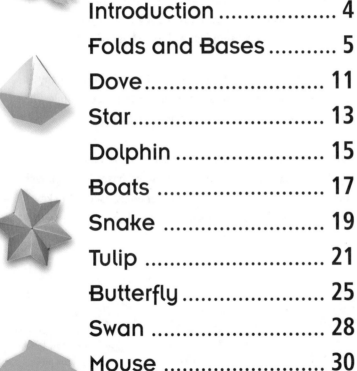

Introduction

Origami, the art of paper folding, has been popular in Japan for hundreds of years and is now loved all around the world. This book shows you how to make lots of great origami models using just a single sheet of paper!

The paper used in origami is thin but strong, so that it can be folded many times. Some of the papers included here are a single, bright shade, while others have beautiful patterns to give your creations an extra lift.

Origami models often share the same folds and basic designs, known as "bases". This introduction explains some of the folds and bases that you will need for the projects in this book. When making the models, follow the key below to find out what the lines and arrows mean. And always crease well!

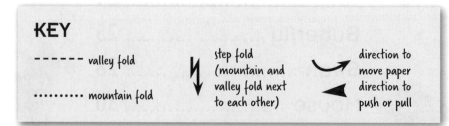

KEY

– – – – – valley fold

·········· mountain fold

step fold (mountain and valley fold next to each other)

direction to move paper

direction to push or pull

Mountain Fold

This simple, central fold is used in many projects.

To make a mountain fold, fold the paper so that the crease is pointing up at you, like a mountain.

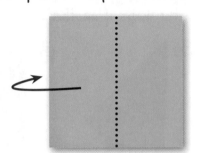 

Valley Fold

The reverse of the mountain fold — carefully match up the edges.

To make a valley fold, fold the paper the other way, so that the crease is pointing away from you, like a valley.

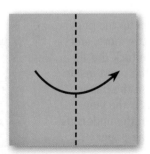 

Inside Reverse Fold

An inside reverse fold is useful if you want to make a nose or a tail, or if you want to flatten the shape of another part of your model.

1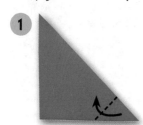

First, fold a piece of paper diagonally in half. Make a valley fold on one point and crease.

2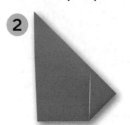

It's important to make sure that the paper is creased well. Run your finger over the crease two or three times.

3

Open

Unfold and then fold the same crease over the other way into a mountain fold. Open up the corner slightly.

4

Open up the paper a little more, and then tuck the tip of the point inside. Close the paper. This is the view from the underside of the paper.

5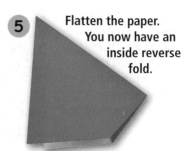

Flatten the paper. You now have an inside reverse fold.

Outside Reverse Fold

An outside reverse fold is useful if you want to make a head, beak, or foot or another part of your model that sticks out.

1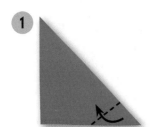

First, fold a piece of paper diagonally in half. Make a valley fold on one point and crease.

2

It's important to make sure that the paper is creased well. Run your finger over the crease two or three times.

3

Open

Unfold and then fold the same crease over the other way into a mountain fold. Open up the corner slightly.

4

Open up the paper a little more and start to turn the corner inside out. Then close the paper when the fold begins to turn.

5

You now have an outside reverse fold. You can either flatten the paper or leave it rounded out.

Kite Base

1

Start with the paper like this.
Valley fold it in half diagonally.

2

Valley fold the left section to
meet the middle crease.

3

Do the same on
the other side.

4

You now
have a
kite base.

Waterbomb Base

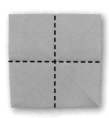

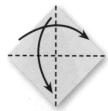

1 Start with a square of paper, like this. Make two diagonal valley folds.

2 The paper should now look like this. Turn it over.

3 Make two valley folds along the horizontal and vertical lines.

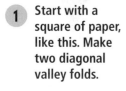

Push   Push

4 Push the paper into this shape, so the middle point pops up.

5 Push the sides in, bringing the back and front sections together.

6 Flatten the paper. You now have a waterbomb base.

Fish Base

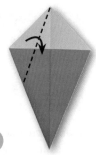

1 Make a kite base, as shown on page 8. Valley fold the left corner.

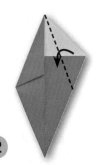

2 Do the same on the other side.

3 The paper should now look like this.

4 Open out the top left corner. Take hold of the inside flap and pull it down to meet the middle crease to make a new flap as shown.

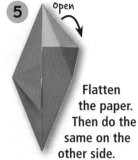

5 Flatten the paper. Then do the same on the other side.

6 You now have a fish base.

Dove

The dove is traditionally used as a symbol of peace and love.
Make your own peace symbol with this origami version!

1 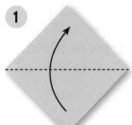 Start with a square of paper in this position, white side up. Valley fold it as shown.

2 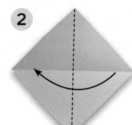 Open the paper out and valley fold it again.

3

Valley fold the left point from left to right.

4

Valley fold the right point from right to left.

5

Open the flap and fold back the right corner. Valley fold on the middle crease.

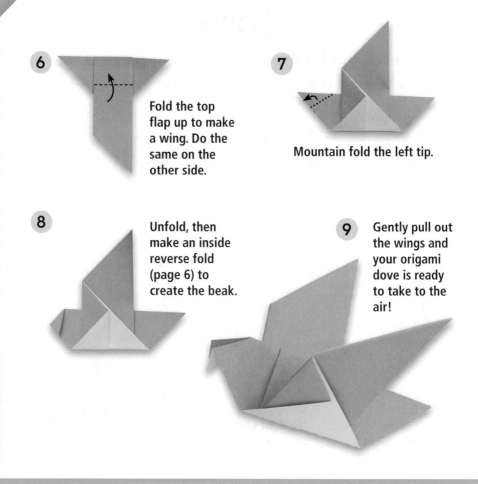

6 Fold the top flap up to make a wing. Do the same on the other side.

7 Mountain fold the left tip.

8 Unfold, then make an inside reverse fold (page 6) to create the beak.

9 Gently pull out the wings and your origami dove is ready to take to the air!

Super star

Perfect to brighten up any celebration, this star looks complicated but it's really easy to make!

1

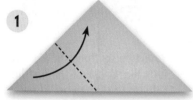

Place your first waterbomb base (page 9) so the open part is at the bottom. Valley fold the left side up to the middle point, crease well and unfold.

2

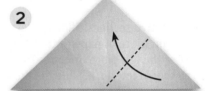

Valley fold the right side up to the middle point, crease well and unfold. Turn over and repeat steps 1 and 2 on the reverse side.

3

You now have one section of your star. Repeat steps 1 and 2 on the five remaining waterbomb bases.

4

Once you have your six sections you are ready to assemble your star.

5

Close-up of interlocking points.

Start with two sections. Slide the left points of the right piece of paper into the right points of the left piece of paper. The two pieces should interlock. Slide the points in as far as they will go.

6

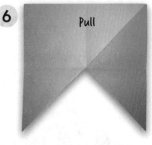

Your two sections should now look like this. Pull the middle fold up to shape your star. Repeat on the reverse.

7

Your two sections should now look like this. Repeat steps 5 and 6 with the remaining sections, adding them one at a time to your sections already added. Finish your star by slotting the last section into the first section, using steps 5 and 6 as a guide.

8

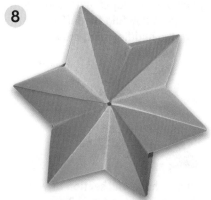

Your star is ready! Use it to decorate parties and special occasions.

Dolphin

Dolphins are supposed to bring good luck to sailors.
Maybe this origami version will do the same for you!

1

Start with a waterbomb base (see page 9). Valley fold the upper flap on the left.

2

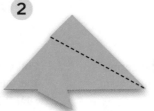

Valley fold the top right section, as shown.

3

Valley fold the top right flap. This will make the fin on the dolphin's back.

4

Valley fold the left side of the paper across the other folds to make a sharp point. This is the nose.

5

Step fold the nose by doing a valley fold and then a mountain fold. This makes it extra pointy!

16

6

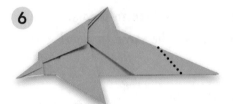

Mountain fold the right corner
so that it points straight down.
This is the tail.

7

Pull out the flap inside
the tail and fold it so
that it points up.

8

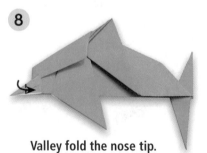

Valley fold the nose tip.

9

Turn your paper over and
you have a sleek dolphin,
complete with fins!

Boats

Even though you cannot put them in the water, you will have lots of fun playing with these origami boats.

1

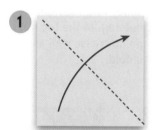

To make a tugboat, valley fold your paper in half diagonally.

2

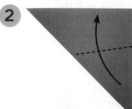

Valley fold the bottom point up at an angle, then turn this fold into an inside reverse fold. See page 6 if you need help.

3

Your paper should look like this. Now valley fold down the top point.

4

Turn this fold into an inside reverse fold to create your boat's cabin.

5

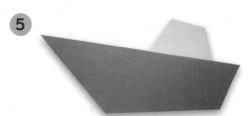

With the hull and cabin complete, your boat is now ready for action.

1

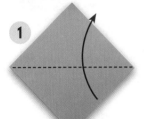

To make a sailboat, valley fold your paper in half diagonally.

2

Valley fold the left point up to the top point, crease well and unfold.

3

Valley fold the right point up to the top point, crease well and unfold.

4

Valley fold the front flap down to the bottom.

5

Mountain fold the back flap down to the bottom of the reverse side.

6

Valley fold the left and right points up again so they meet in the middle.

7

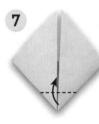

Valley fold the bottom point up to create a stand for your boat.

8

Turn your sailboat around. It is ready to use now.

Snake

Follow these simple steps to make this patterned origami snake.
The wavy folds create a slithering, snake-like movement.

1

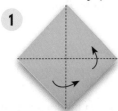

Start with your paper
like this. Make two
diagonal valley folds.

2

Valley fold the top and
bottom corners to meet
in the middle.

3

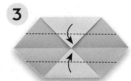

Valley fold the top and
bottom sections to
meet in the middle.

4 Repeat step 3.

5 The paper should
now look like this.

6

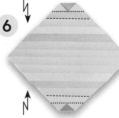

Unfold and turn the
paper over. Then start
to make a series of
step folds inward
from both ends.

7 Continue to
step fold. A
pattern like
this should
appear.

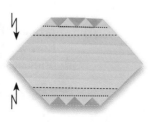

8

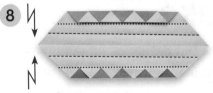

Repeat step 7.

9

From the left, count in two and a half diamonds. Mountain fold the paper back on that line.

10

Unfold the last fold you made. Now mountain fold the bottom section back behind the top section.

11

Use this crease

Using the crease on the left that you made in step 9, make an outside reverse fold (page 7).

12

Mountain fold the top left corner.

13

Unfold, then make an outside reverse fold to create the snake's head.

14

Make alternate mountain and valley folds along the body.

15

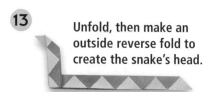

Arrange the model like this. Now you have a zigzagging origami snake!

t>21<>21

21<

Tulip

This tulip may be tricky to get right, but it is very pretty and will make a lovely gift for someone special.

1

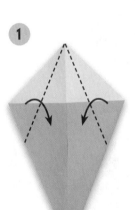

To make the stem and leaf, choose green paper. Valley fold the left and right sides to the middle.

2

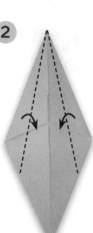

Valley fold the left and right sides again to the middle.

3

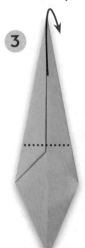

Mountain fold your model in half horizontally.

4

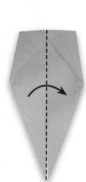

Valley fold the left side over to the right, crease well and then unfold.

5 Unfold the mountain fold from step 3. Turn your model over so it looks like the picture in step 6.

6 Mountain fold the top sides of your paper to shape a leaf for your stem. Use your fingers to crease the paper and give shape to your leaf.

7 Valley fold the bottom point up to complete your stem.

8 Your model should now stand up. Put it to one side while you make your flower.

9

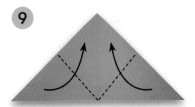

To make the petals, choose pink, red, or yellow paper. Place your waterbomb base (page 9) with the point at the top. Valley fold the top left and right points up into the middle.

10

Valley fold the top right flap over to the left.

11

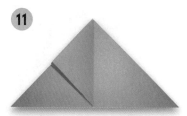

Your paper should now look like this. Turn it over and repeat steps 9 and 10 on the reverse.

12

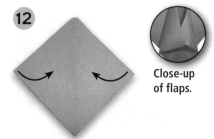

Close-up of flaps.

Take the top left and right flaps and slot the right flap into the pocket of the left flap as far as you can.

13

Your model should look like this. Carefully press down to flatten the paper, making sure the sides are equal.

14

Your model should look like this. Turn it over and repeat steps 12 and 13 on the reverse.

15

Hold here

Blow here

Your model should look like this. Blow gently into the bottom end to inflate your tulip.

16

Your model should now look like this. Gently pull back the top layers to create petals.

17

Your model should now look like this.

18

To finish your tulip, carefully place your flower on the finished stem from step 8. Isn't it pretty?

Butterfly

A butterfly's wings have symmetrical markings. Use the patterned paper to create a real fluttering beauty.

1

Start with the paper white side up. Valley fold it in half and open it up. Then valley fold it in half the other way and open it again.

2

Valley fold the paper diagonally and open it up. Fold it diagonally the other way and open it again.

3

Valley fold the top right corner. Fold the other corners in the same way.

4

Valley fold the top right corner again.

5

Fold the other corners in the same way.

6

You should now have a small square, like this.

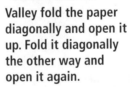

7

Unfold your paper completely. Valley fold the right section.

8

Valley fold the left section to meet in the middle.

9

Your paper should now look like this.

10

Take the top corners and gently pull them open, so that the top folds down.

11

Keep pulling the corners out and bringing the top down, so that this shape appears.

12

Flatten the paper as shown. Then turn it so that the top becomes the bottom.

13

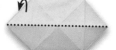

Repeat steps 10 and 11 to get the shape in this picture. Mountain fold the top back.

14

Valley fold the upper right flap.

15

Do the same on the other side.

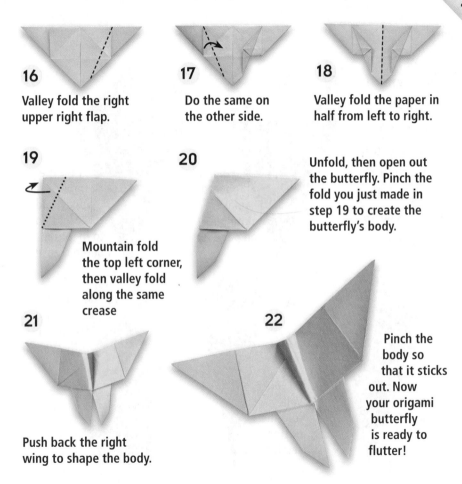

16

Valley fold the right upper right flap.

17

Do the same on the other side.

18

Valley fold the paper in half from left to right.

19

Mountain fold the top left corner, then valley fold along the same crease

20

Unfold, then open out the butterfly. Pinch the fold you just made in step 19 to create the butterfly's body.

21

Push back the right wing to shape the body.

22

Pinch the body so that it sticks out. Now your origami butterfly is ready to flutter!

Swan

There are few more elegant sights than a graceful swan gliding across a lake. Here's how to make one.

1 Find out how to make a kite base on page 8.

2 Turn the paper over. Valley fold the right edge to meet the middle crease.

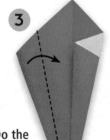

3 Do the same on the other side.

4 Valley fold the bottom section up.

5 Fold down the tip at the top. This will be the swan's head.

6

Mountain fold along the middle crease so that the left side folds behind the right.

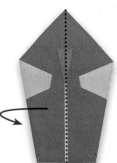

7 Now turn your paper sideways so that it looks like this. Pull up the neck as shown.

Pull

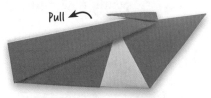

8

Pull

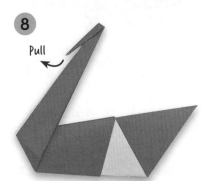

Flatten the paper and then pull the head into position.

9

Now you have a beautiful swan. Try placing it on water and see if it floats!

Mouse

The mouse investigates its surroundings with a long,
pointy nose – just like this origami version!

1

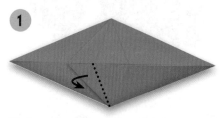

Find out how to make a fish base on
page 10. Turn it so that the flaps are
pointing to the left. Mountain fold the
bottom flap and tuck it under itself.

2

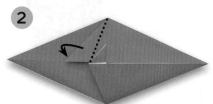

Mountain fold the top flap and
tuck it under the bottom flap.

3

Mountain fold the left point.

4

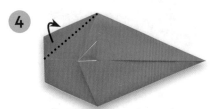

Mountain fold the top
left corner.

5

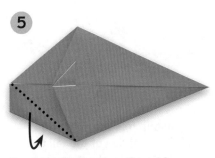

Do the same on the other side.

6

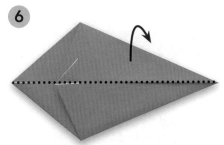

Mountain fold in half, so that the top section folds down behind the bottom section.

7

Valley fold the front flap. Then do the same to the back flap to create the ears.

8

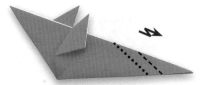

Mountain fold the right point and then valley fold to make a step fold.

9

Unfold and do an inside reverse fold (page 6) to make the tail point downward, as shown. Then do a second inside reverse fold to tuck the tail back up.

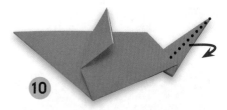

10

Mountain fold the right edge of the front flap of the tail to tuck it in and make it narrow. Do the same for the back flap.

Pull

11

Open out the ears and pull the tail down gently.

12

You now have an inquisitive origami mouse, complete with a pointy nose and tail!

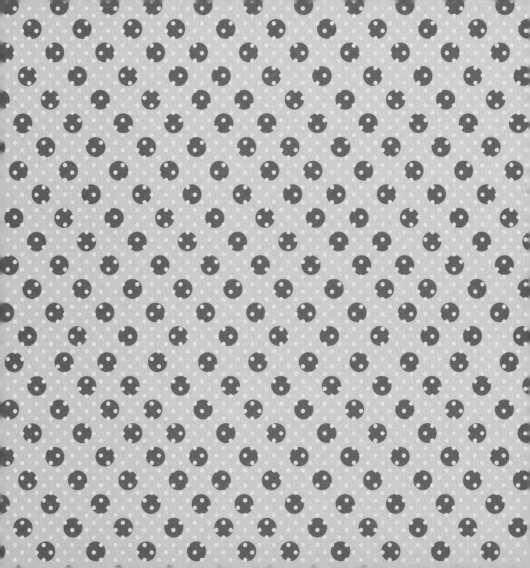

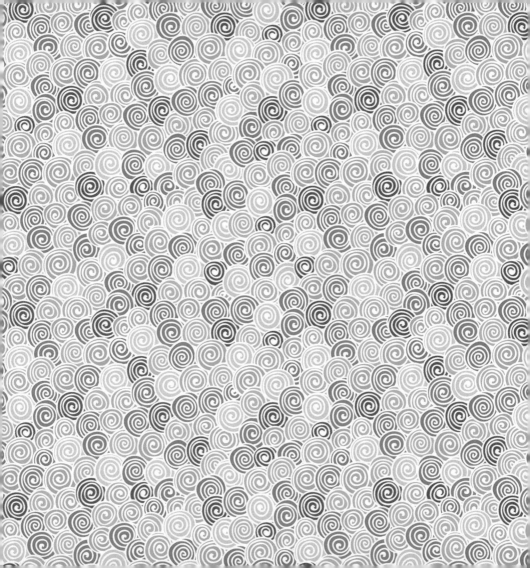

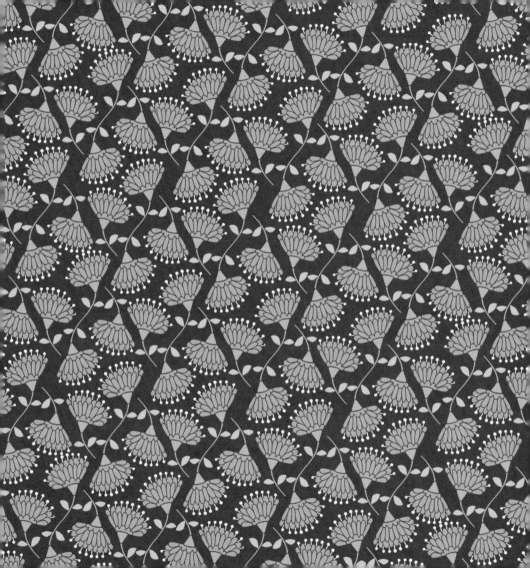

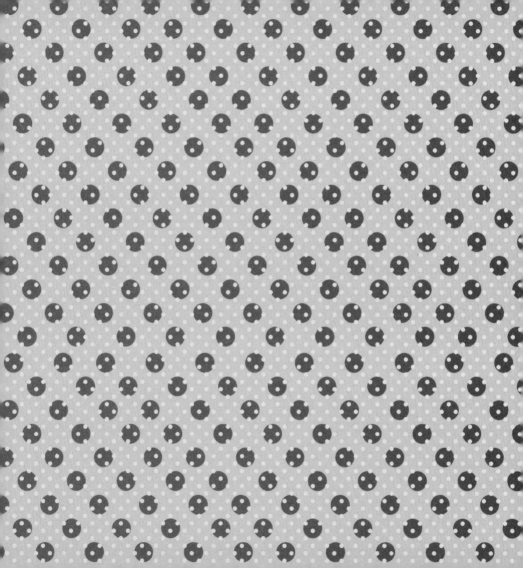

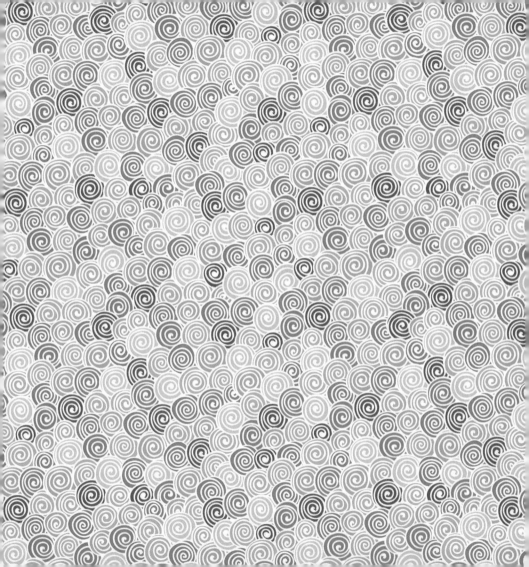

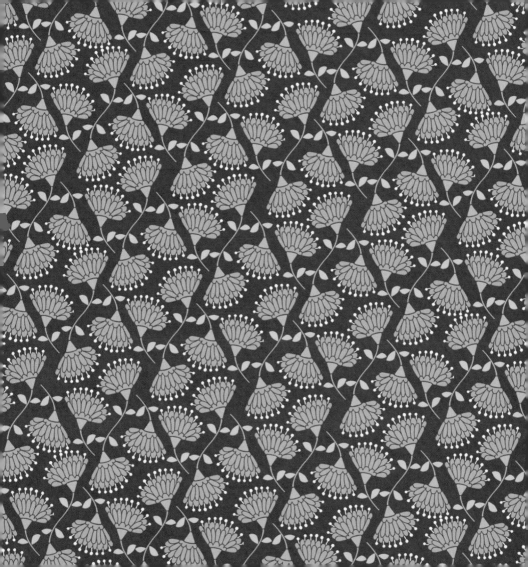

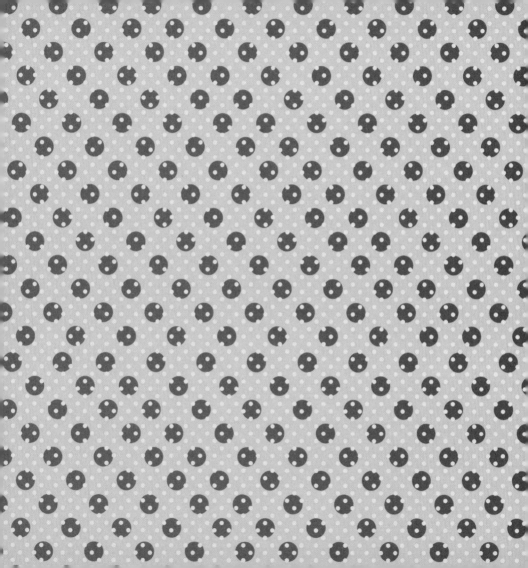

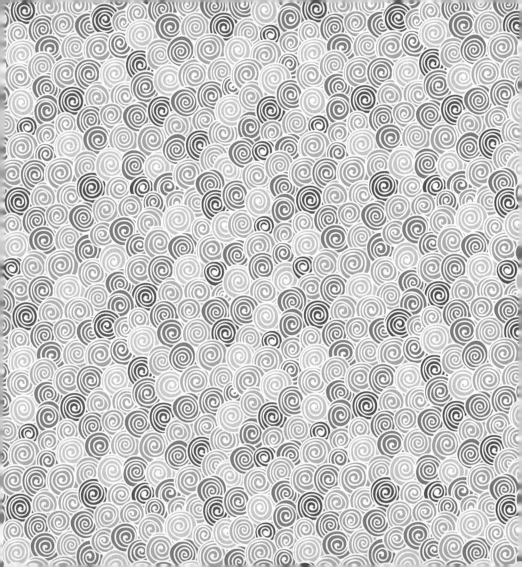

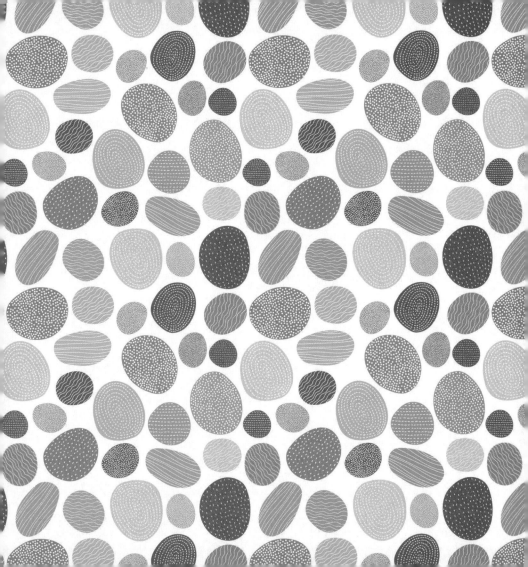

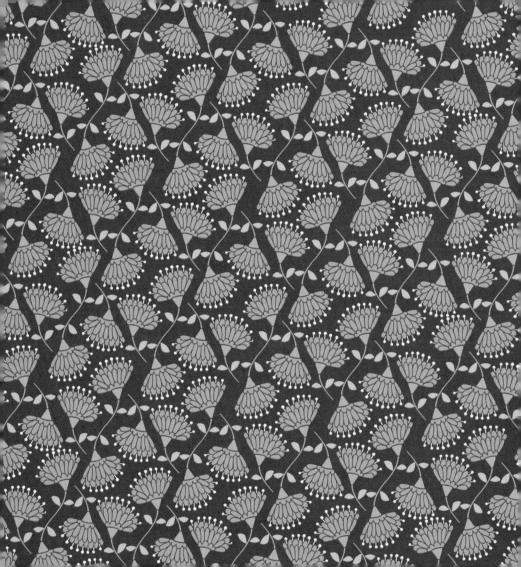

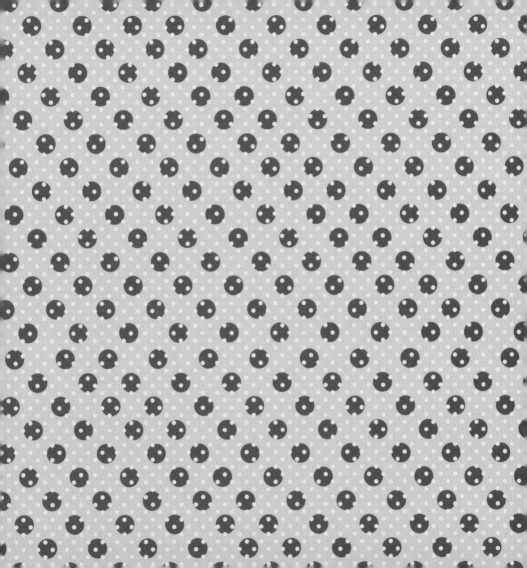

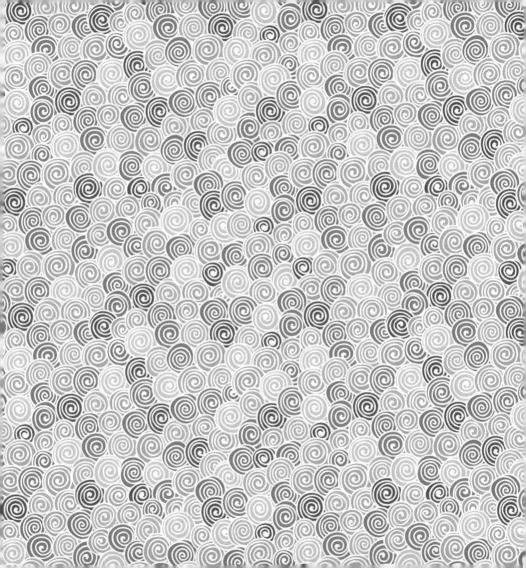

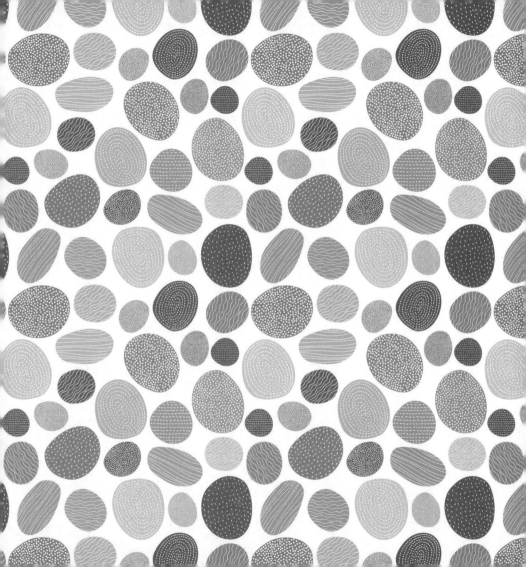

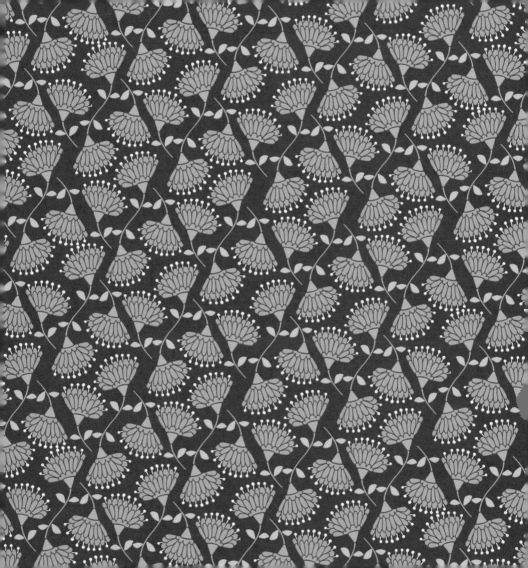

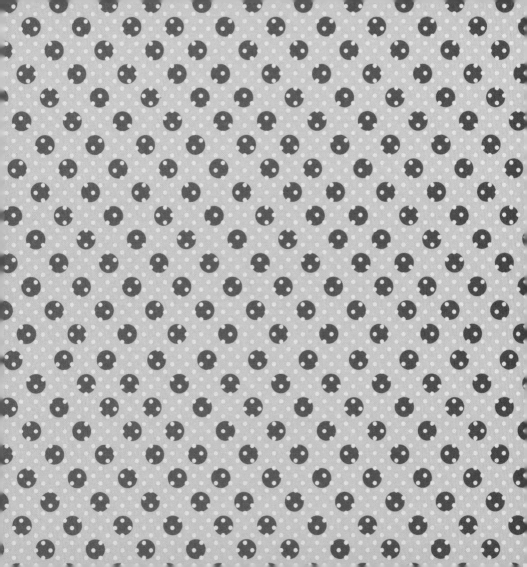

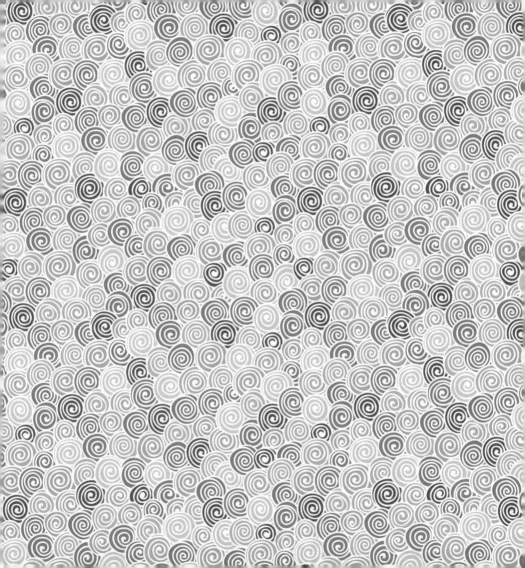

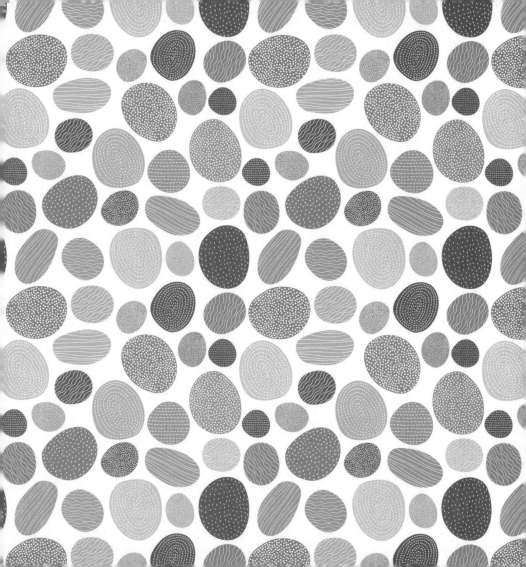

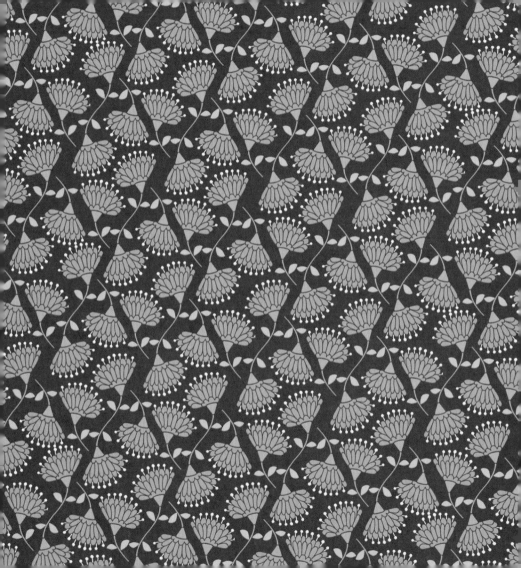

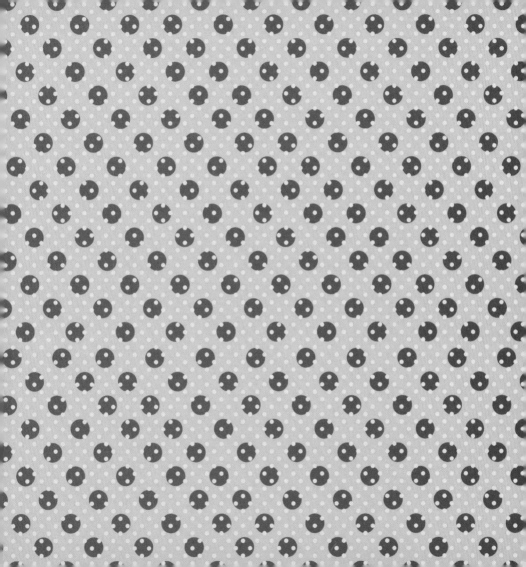

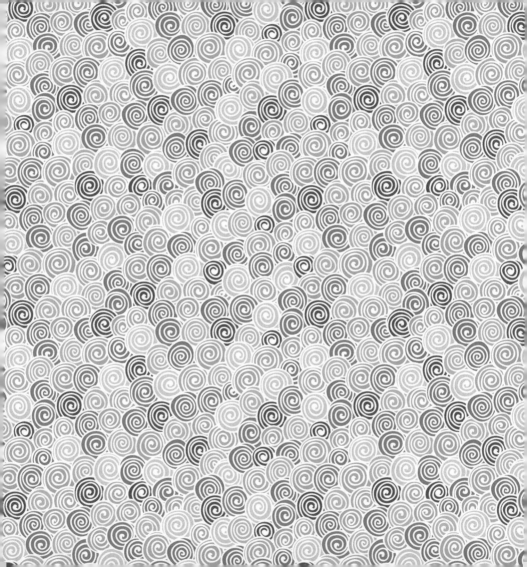

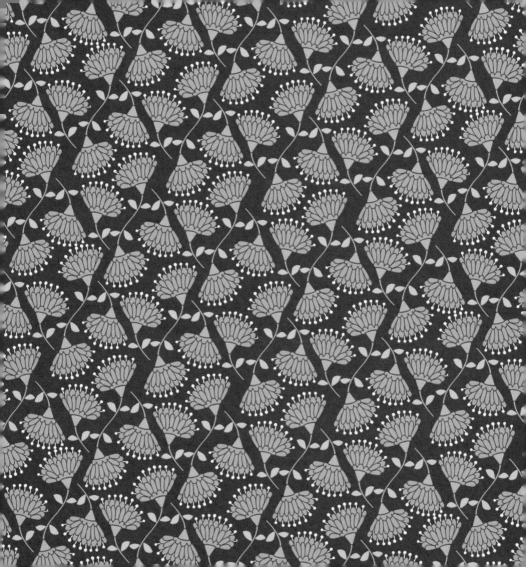

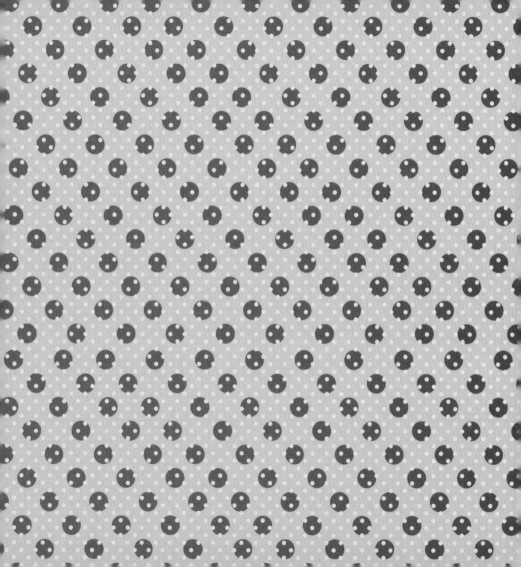

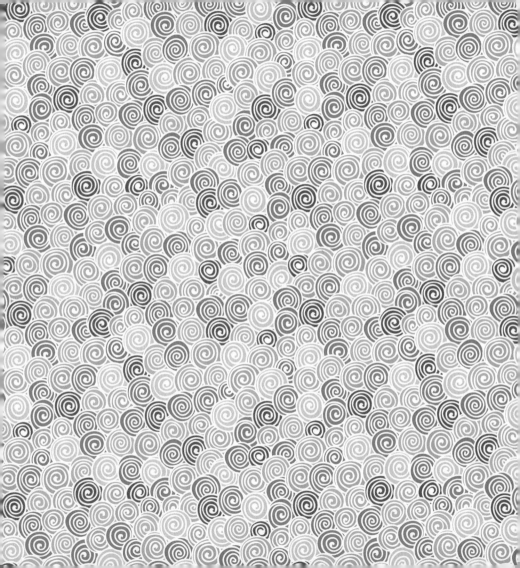

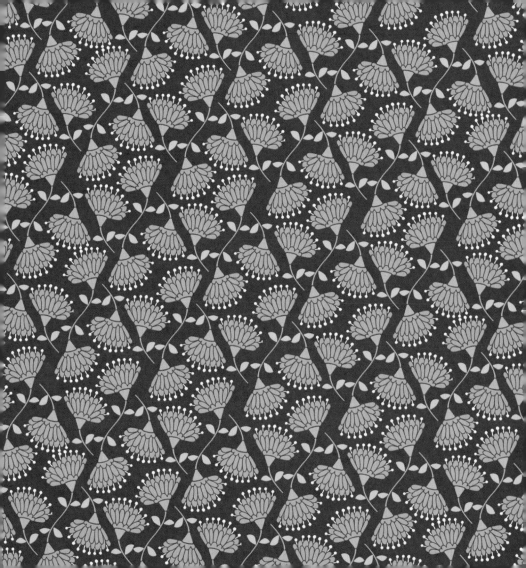

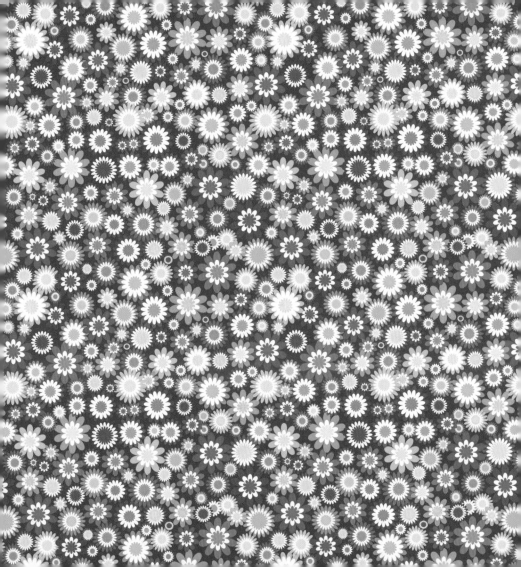

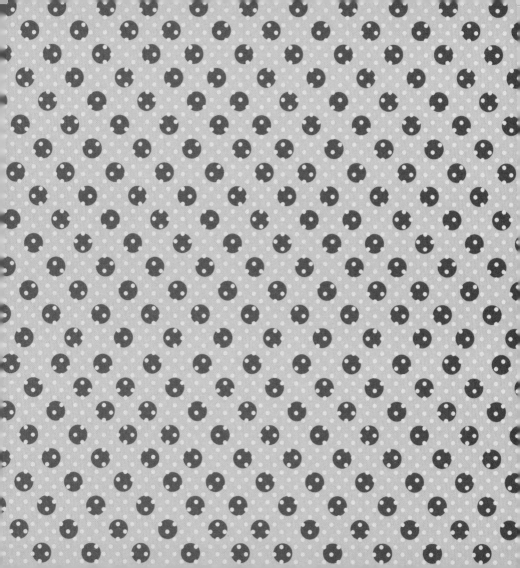

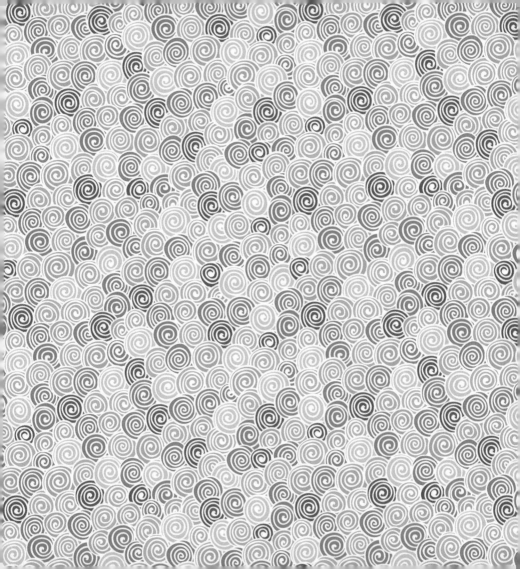

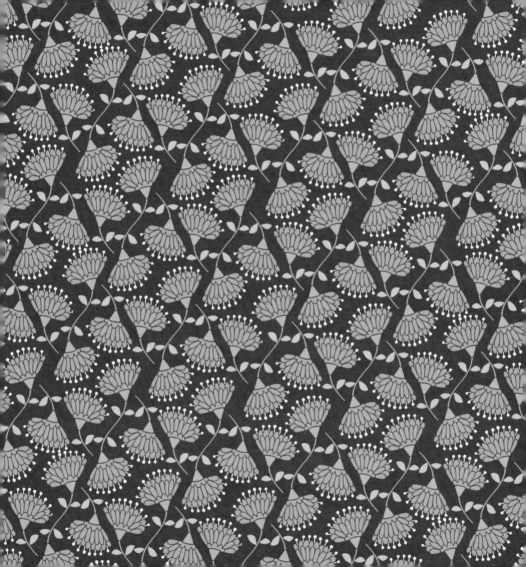

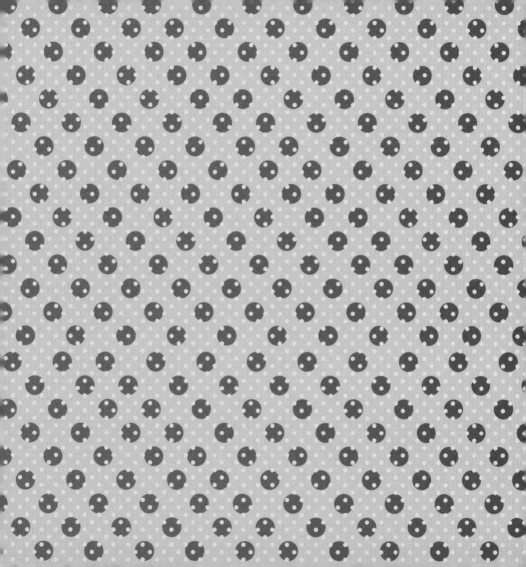

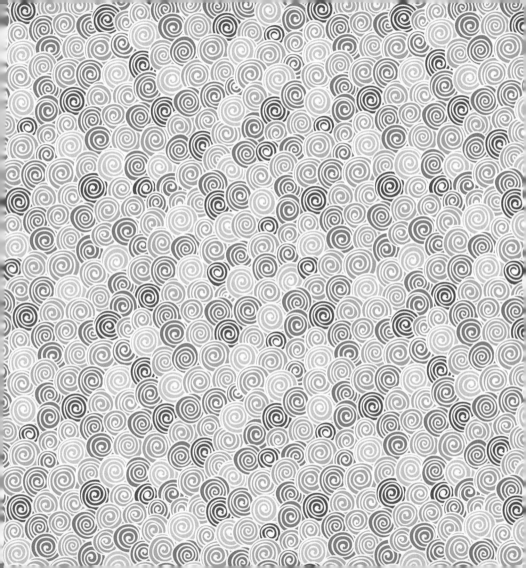

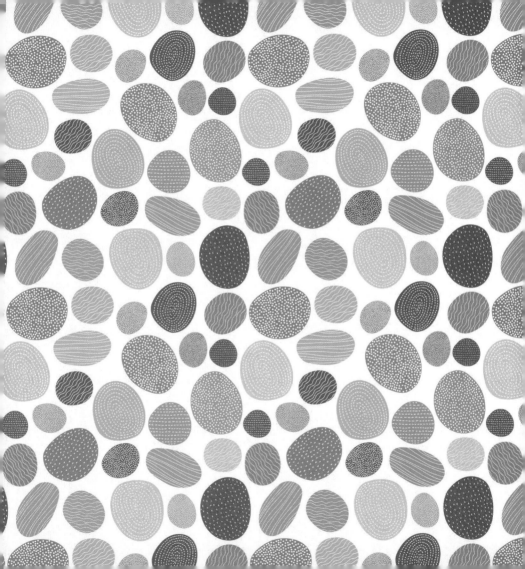

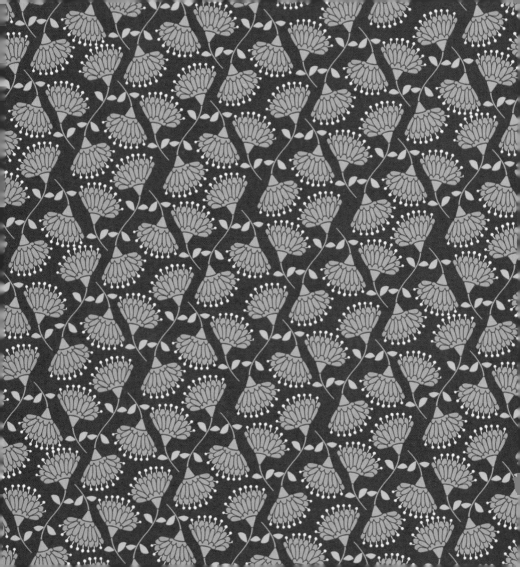

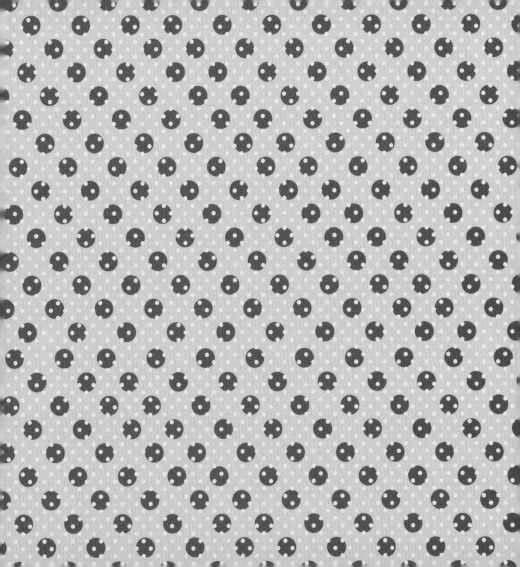

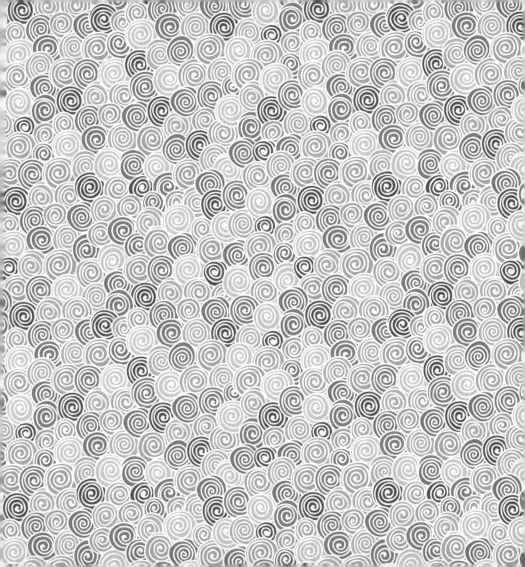

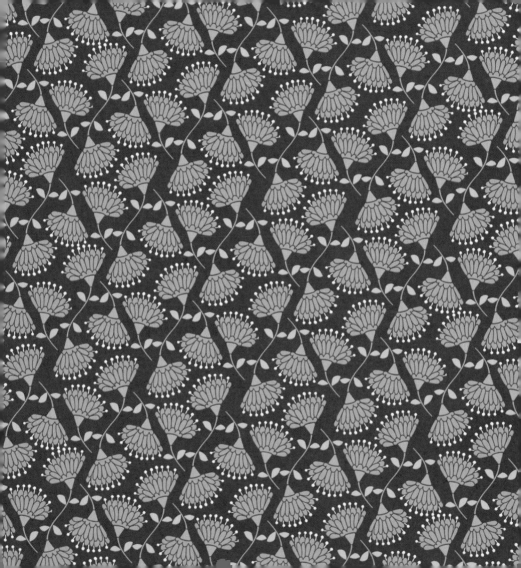

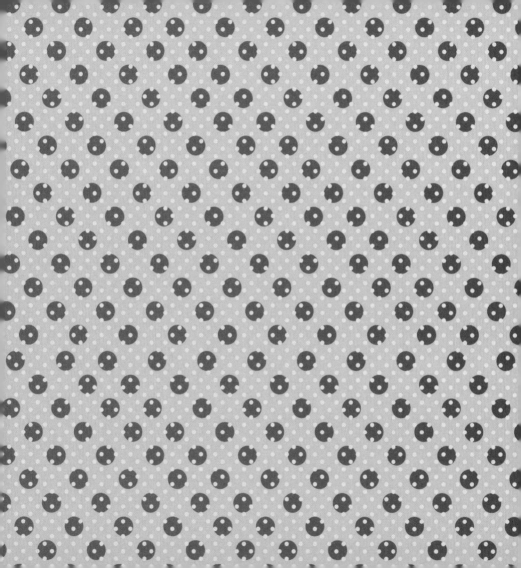

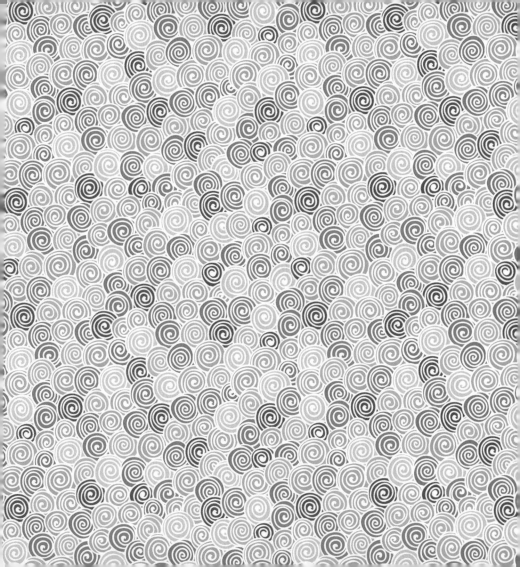

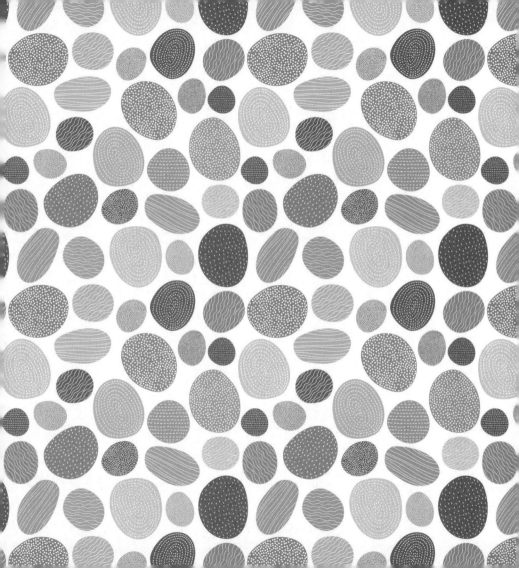

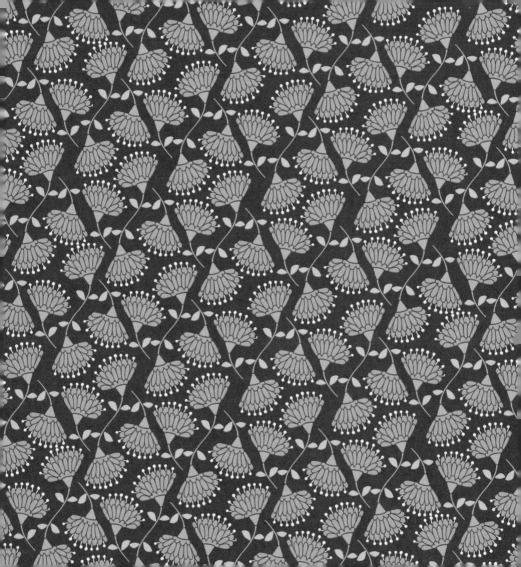

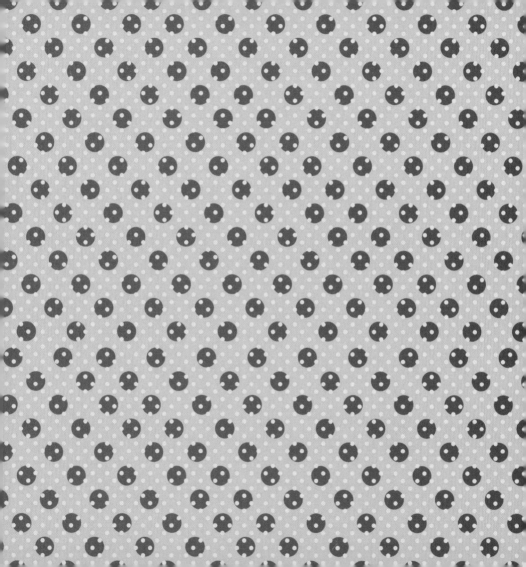

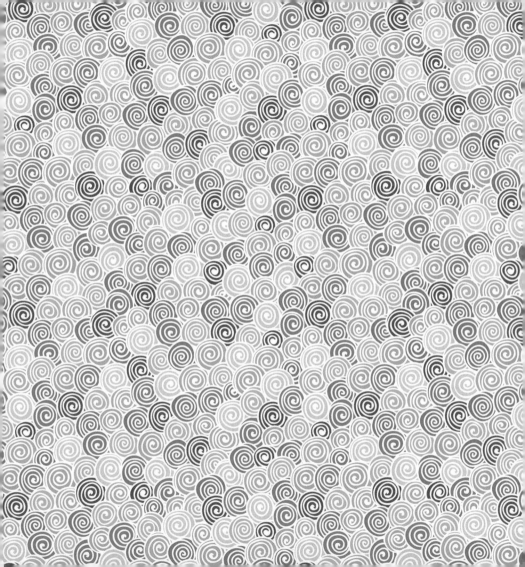

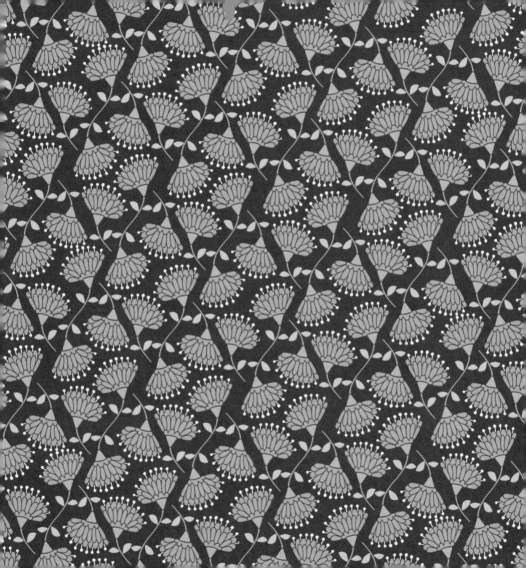

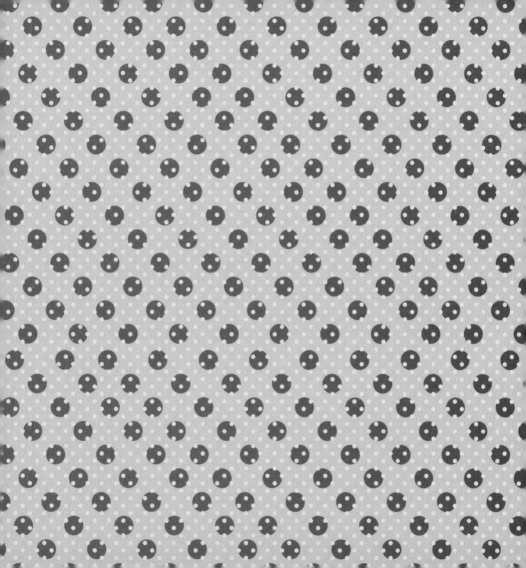

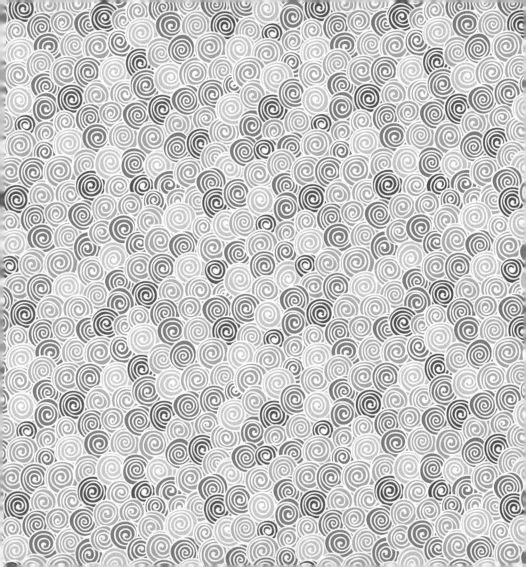

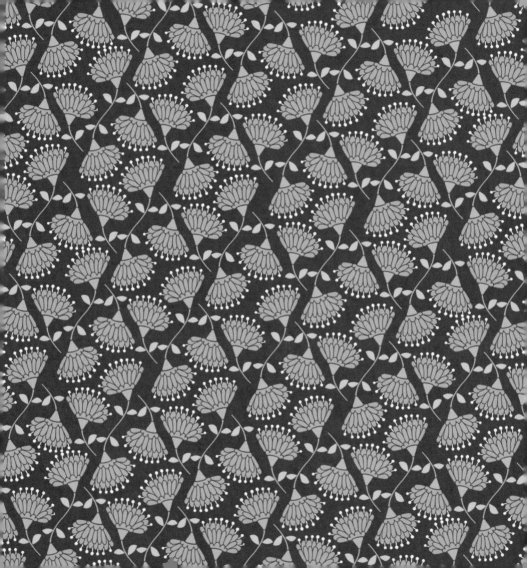

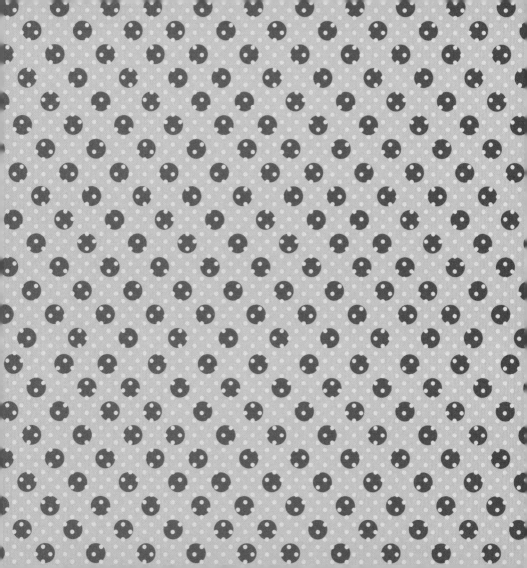

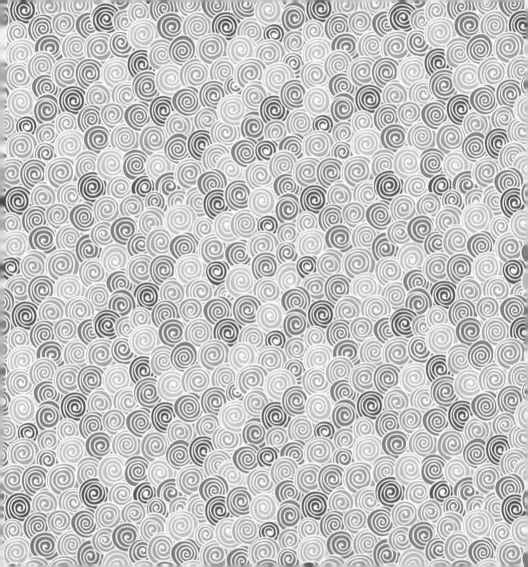

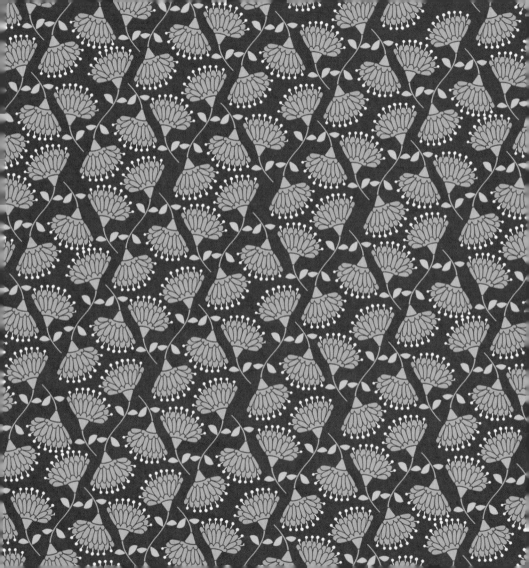

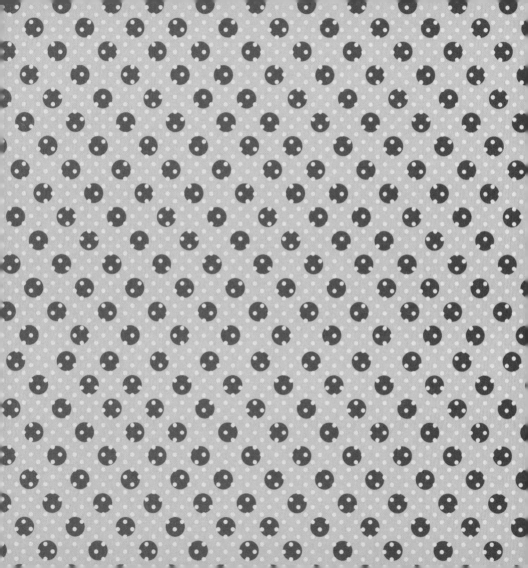

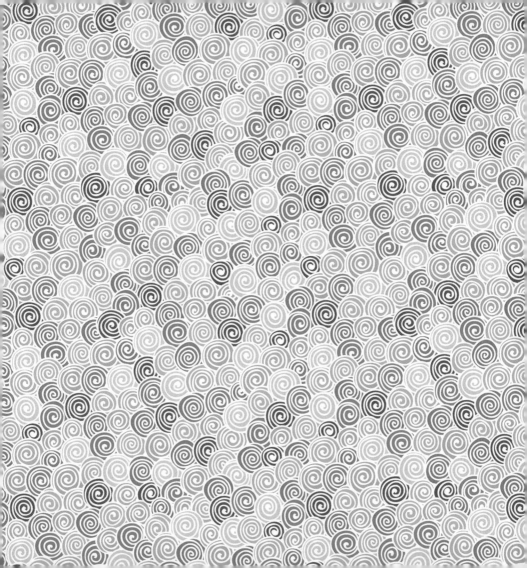

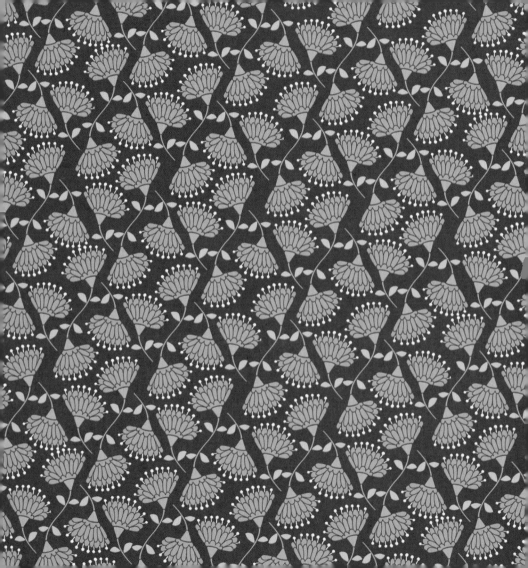

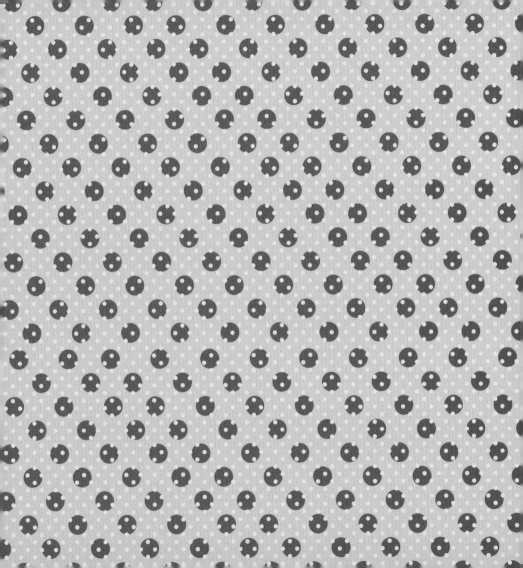

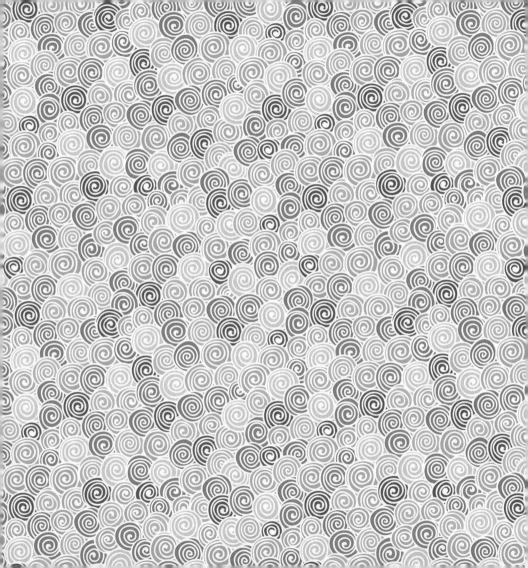

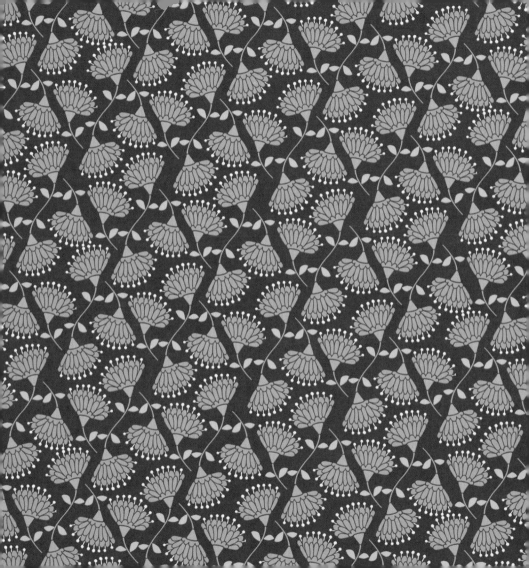

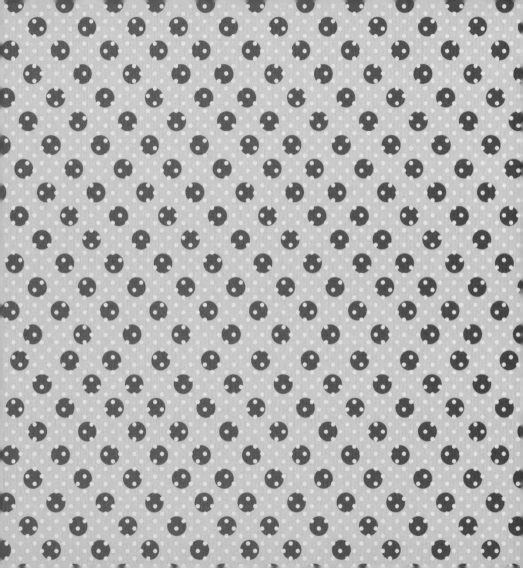

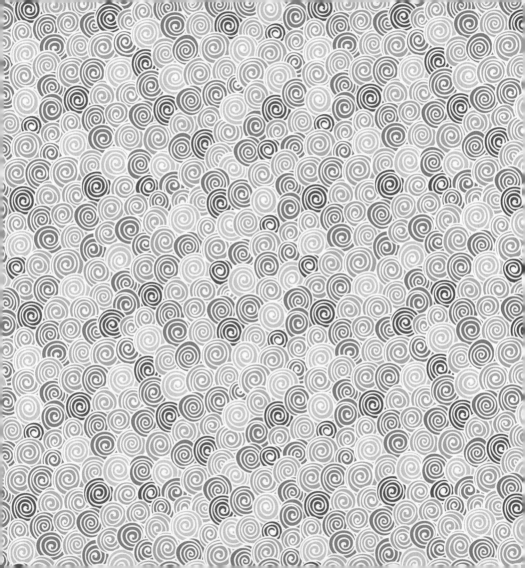

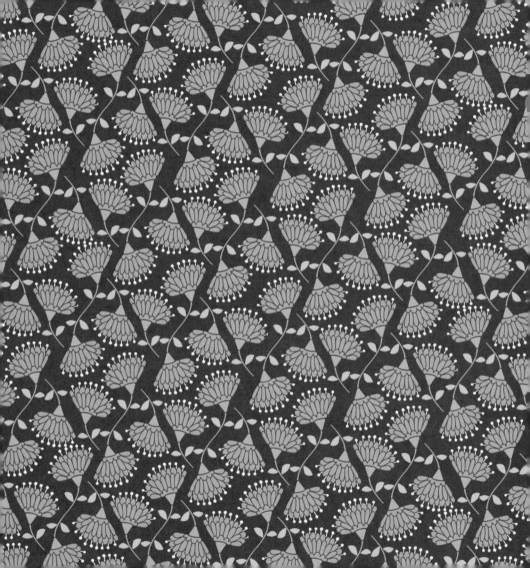

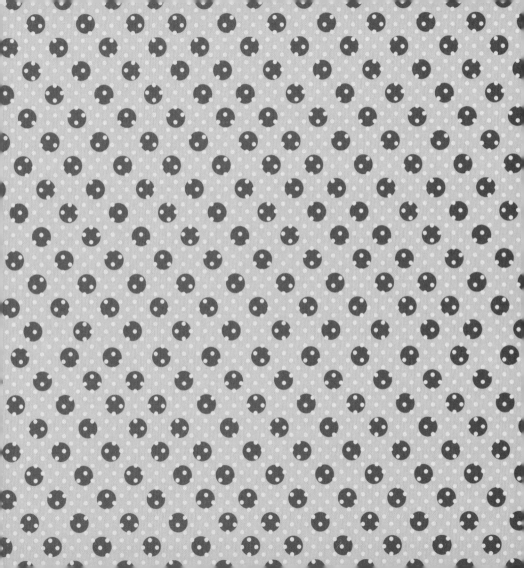

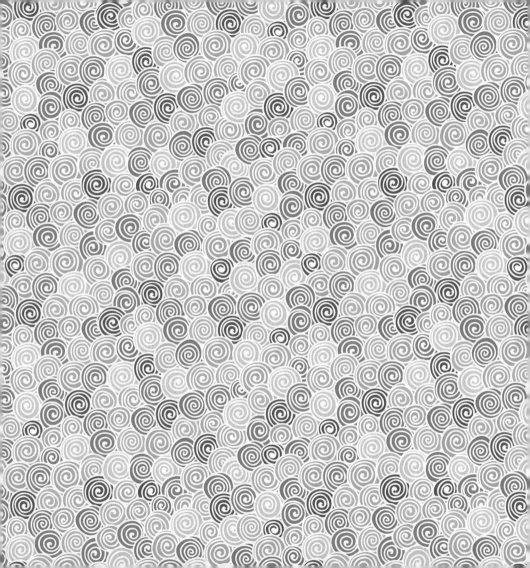

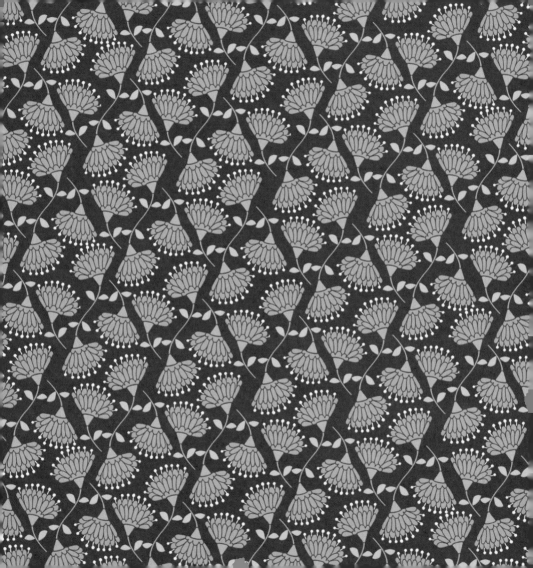

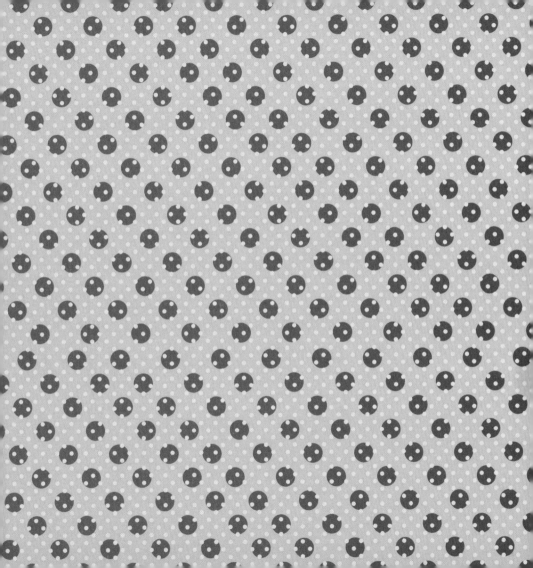